Colleen Moore, among Filmdom's all-time "greats"

Terry Pierce

Colleen Moore's Fairy Castle

☆ ☆ ☆

"For the young at heart"

☆ ☆ ☆ ☆ ☆

Colleen Moore's Lilliputian castle for Fairyland characters, with Cinderella appropriately as its Princess, is a splendid reflection of the personality of its creator, whom the Chicago SUN-TIMES in a review of her fabulous career described as:—

"The quixotic pixie of motion pictures. The girl with one blue eye and one brown eye. An American Shamrock with a Dutch bob. The star of 'Flaming Youth.' The winsome lass of 'Lilac Time.' A grown-up Alice in Wonderland . . . Youth, romance, glamour, and charm . . . That was Colleen Moore."

←⫷ *The Chapel, impressive in its ecclesiastical splendor*

Miss Moore placing Cinderella's coach in courtyard

"A CASTLE RIGHT OUT OF FAIRYLAND"

"Almost all children know that fairy castles do exist. They have seen them in their dreams and, once in a fleeting while, even when they're awake. For those few children who don't believe in them— or haven't been lucky enough to see one—there is a real-honest-to-goodness fairy castle in Chicago. It's the Colleen Moore Fairy Castle, and it's as breath-taking as any fairy castle that ever brightened the world of make-believe.

"... More than 700 artists and craftsmen combined their talents on the nine-year job of building and decorating this beautiful palace at a cost of almost half a million dollars.

"... It is a free exhibit at Chicago's Museum of Science and Industry where thousands enjoy it each year. It is dedicated to those children (and older folk, too) who believe that fairy castles do exist."

—*Extract from FAMILY WEEKLY MAGAZINE*

← *The Great Hall and its floating staircase*

Battersea enamel wine keg

Prince Charming's golden sword

Set of Royal Doulton china

Colleen Moore's Fairy Castle, one of the most popular attractions of Chicago's world-famed Museum of Science and Industry and with more than a million spellbound viewers a year, is the fulfillment of a childhood dream.

Explaining the beginning of this dream, Miss Moore said, "We lived in the South and the skies were very beautiful there. At sunset I used to lie on the grass and look at the billowy clouds floating in a sea of gold, and I was quite sure that on one of those white clouds was a wonderful castle belonging to a fairy princess. It was a rare and splendid palace with furniture of gold and silver. The chandeliers were hung with diamonds. A great hall was filled with treasures that belonged to the fairy folk. The floor of the drawing room was made of strawberry ice cream."

The Fairy Castle had its beginning when Miss Moore's father, Charles Morrison, made a doll house for her when she was two years old. From then until she was grown up, she had seven doll houses, each nicer than the one before. On her seventh birthday her father gave her a gilt box. It was just an inch square

*Postage stamp-sized
dictionary*

Thimble-size bejeweled clock

*Typical Fairyland
chest of drawers*

*Bureau adorned with
Japanese fairytales*

and had a magnifying glass on the cover. Inside was a wee red book, a dictionary with words in such fine print that they could be read only with the glass. This little dictionary, now reposing on a lectern in the library of the Fairy Castle, was the start of her miniature collection.

Years later, when the collection had grown to a filled cabinet and Miss Moore was a famous motion picture star in Hollywood, she took a trip to Honolulu with her father. Enroute they talked about their favorite subjects—miniatures and doll houses—and it was on this trip that a Fairy Castle to house the collection was born. Mr. Morrison said, "This time, get an architect, engage artists and build that fairy castle you have always talked about."

Horace Jackson, a well-known architect who designed the sets at the First National Studios in Hollywood, was enchanted with the idea. In designing the house, Mr. Jackson's idea was to keep away from any true period of architecture so that the Fairy Castle would look as if it had stepped out of an illustration in a fairy tale book.

The Library's decorations recall the stories of Gulliver, Robinson Crusoe and Captain Kidd

Thumbnail Bible, no bigger than a wedding ring

WORTH A HALF MILLION DOLLARS

The little palace measures nine feet square and its highest tower stands twelve feet above the floor. It has its own electrical and plumbing systems with running water in the bathrooms and the kitchen. It is made of aluminum so it will last and because of its lightness. Structurally, it has 200 pieces that come apart and it contains over 1,000 wee treasures. With its many treasures, it has been estimated that the Fairy Castle is worth a half million dollars.

Chief advisor, enthusiast and engineer in making this fabulous showpiece a reality was Colleen's father, assisted by master technician, Jerry Rouleau. It also reflects the creative and artistic genius of Harold Grieve, a decorator responsible for many homes in Hollywood and New York. In designing the interior of the Castle, Mr. Grieve went on the premise that the Fairy Princess who lived in it liked to collect antiques, so he and Colleen went all over seeking out those things that could have belonged to the fairy folk.

In their quest they found Sleeping Beauty's bed, King Arthur's Round Table, Hans Brinker's silver skates, and countless other treasures. All the well-known

fairy tales are represented by something in the Castle, and the colorful way in which everything has been presented impresses on spectators, young and old, that it is the miniature replica of a fascinating dream house and not a place where mortals could live.

When asked what period furniture he had used in the Castle, Mr. Grieve says, "It is Early Fairy."

George Townsend Cole, celebrated mural artist, did the glittering walls in the living room and Bayard de Volo made the floors which, with their fairy carving and gold and silver inlay, seem too heavenly for mortal feet.

Many of Miss Moore's other artist friends contributed their talents, inspired by the thrill of aiding in the creation of such an unusual masterpiece. But, rather than dwell on this long list of illustrious collaborators, let us take a trip through its magic halls and see for ourselves the wonders brought into being by the genius of these marvelous craftsmen.

THE GREAT CENTRAL HALL

Let's save the garden and the Castle's exterior for the last and start in the great central hall. That's the room in which we see Miss Moore in the picture shown on page one. Since she looks a trifle cramped, let us pretend that we have shrunk into Lilliputians before we start our tour.

Now, having reduced yourself to an imaginary five inches, let's march boldly into the Great Hall. Here you are walking on fine ivory carved with little rose vines, a motif that carries on up to the great golden pillars far overhead. Two stories above are the beautiful painted domes, painted by Helga Brabon, where the fairy folk of Grimm and Hans Christian Andersen again go through their adventures.

On the walls hang many paintings. You'll see Alice and her many friends from Wonderland; a painting by Willy Pogany; and another of Snow White, painted by Lisbeth Stone Barret and given to Miss Moore by Marguerite Clark, who was a famous actress when Miss Moore was a young girl. Miss Clark had posed for this very picture, which depicts her most famous role.

←⫷ *Stained glass windows enhance the Chapel's beauty*

Cinderella's story inspired the Drawing Room's murals

Grain-of-wheat lights illuminate the diamond chandelier

There are also paintings of Miss Moore by Leon Gordon showing her in the Alice Blue gown from her picture, "Irene," and a portrait of the Fairy Princess by Frank Lackner that was posed for by Miss Moore's daughter, Judy Hargrave Coleman.

Elsewhere about the Great Hall are paintings in miniature size by James Montgomery Flagg, Arthur William Brown, Hubert Stowitts, Frederick Haynes of Canada, and Hugo Balin. Because the only fairy tales many modern children know are those they see in the movies and the funny papers, George McManus, an old friend of Colleen, painted a picture depicting "Jiggs," his famous comic character, as Old King Cole; and Percy Crosby painted "Skippy" in a suit of armor. Similarly, the movies are represented by a water color by the famous Walt Disney showing "Mickey" and "Minnie Mouse" in the roles of the King and Queen of Hearts.

Aside from the wonders of its ceilings and walls, the Great Hall is also a fairyland museum with treasures gathered from all corners of the earth where the wee folks dwell.

It is here you will find the Goose that laid the golden eggs resting on a table fashioned of gold and enamel and with a gold mesh basket holding several golden eggs beside her. Nearby is the singing harp Jack stole from the wicked giant who lived at the top of the beanstalk. And, under a glass bell on a little rosewood table stand the chairs of the Three Bears. Each chair rests on the head of a pin. The largest chair weighs only 150,000th of an ounce.

Next to these are Hans Brinker's silver skates and Cinderella's glass slippers. These little slippers are slightly over one-quarter of an inch long, are hollow, and have tiny red glass bows. Miss Moore looked far and wide to find a glass blower who could blow these hollow slippers for her, even going to Venice, Italy, the world's center of the glass blowing craft, where she was told they could not be blown hollow. You can imagine her gratification, therefore, when in Jackson, Michigan, her quest was ended when she discovered E. H. Rohl, a skilled artisan who proved able to produce just the kind of slippers Cinderella lost rushing back from her storied ball.

Elsewhere in this chamber is a finely carved ivory table that holds a tiny dueling pistol which really shoots silver bullets; and on a rack nearby hangs a perfect scale reproduction of an early American musket. On a silver table rests the crowns of the Prince and Princess. Near the Princess' crown, which is made of pearls set in gold with a tiny green emerald cut in the shape of a shamrock in the center, is a fairy wand, with a diamond in its star; while next to the Prince's gold crown, set with rubies and sapphires, lies his scepter inset with matching gems.

Ranged along the wall on the opposite side are still other treasures including a carved ivory cabinet housing a collection of miniature snuff bottles, and another cabinet holding an ivory statuette of the Goose Boy of Sparta.

Tall, etched glass windows overlooking the garden tell the story of Jack and the Beanstalk, Prince Charming, and the Princess and the Seven Swans; and over the doorway leading to the garden is sculptured the story of the Pied Piper of Hamlin. Two silver-armored knights that once belonged to Rudolph Valentino stand on either side of the doorway. These rare museum pieces are invaluable. Even we, diminutive as we are, must not risk touching them with clumsy fingers. Little red ropes attached to bronze posts guard these fragile masterpieces against possible damage from some careless fairy who might brush by in his excitement to climb that wonderful stairway to your left.

It would scarcely seem possible that any but fairy feet could flit up these tiny steps; but presently we will try, for we will want to see the beautiful rooms at the top.

First, however, let's turn to the right. In doing so, don't knock over that alabaster jar. It came from the Tomb of the Kings in the Valley of the Nile, and once held kohl for some Egyptian Princess to paint her eyelashes. On the other side is a porcelain urn from Thailand; it is over 1,000 years old.

THE DRAWING ROOM

We now pause in the archway leading to the Drawing Room. The floor is of rose quartz with a border of green jade. Made in China, it took nine months to complete. It seems almost to shimmer with beauty. Perhaps, its glistening surface catches some reflection of the enchanting ceiling above it—misty clouds in a sea-blue sky—or, perhaps, it catches the light from that indescribably lovely diamond, emerald and pearl chandelier which hangs with delicate grace in the middle of the room. Even as we look, it suddenly is bathed in added brilliance. Electric light bulbs, the size of a grain of wheat, light up and are reflected a thousand times in the glittering facets of the jewels. The chandelier, itself, is a gem. This little masterpiece was designed and created by H. B. Crouch, a jeweler and famous authority on antiques. Many of Miss Moore's personal jewels were used to make this a true fairy gem.

On the walls of this room are murals telling the story of Cinderella. They were painted by George Townsend Cole, who also painted the glowing ceiling. In one corner is the fireplace. The andirons are silver and, if you hold your breath, you can hear the ticking of the tiny gold clock, set with diamonds and emeralds, on the chimney ledge. Even in Fairyland you must know what the time is, and this wee timepiece is wound daily, ticking the hour for Cinderella to leave the ball.

The furniture is of silver, except the grand piano which is of rosewood with legs of ivory. The manuscripts on the piano were handwritten by the composers,

King Arthur's round table dominates the palatial dining room (next page) ⇒→

themselves, at Miss Moore's request. They include Rachmaninoff's famous "Prelude"; "Rhapsody in Blue," by George Gershwin; and "Firebird Suite," by Stravinsky. Our popular musicians are represented by "Alexander's Ragtime Band," by Irving Berlin; "Oh! What A Beautiful Morning," by Richard Rodgers; and "Over There," by George M. Cohen. Carrie Jacobs Bond wrote "The End of A Perfect Day," and Charles Wakefield Cadman is represented by "From the Land of the Sky Blue Water."

The little ivory table in this room is unique, as are the ivory chessmen that occupy it. They comprise one of the smallest sets in the world and are perfect in every detail. There is also a silver secretary holding an ivory statuette of William Tell, and opposite it a "Hickory Dickory" grandfather clock.

A pair of intricately carved pillars telling the stories of German fairy tales stand on either side of a concealed staircase leading to the upper floor.

Over the door to the dining room is a heraldic shield. It shows the date, 1928, the year the first casting was made for the Fairy Castle. On either side of the doorway is an amber vase more than 500 years old that once belonged to the Dowager Empress of China.

KING ARTHUR'S DINING HALL

The raftered ceiling of the long Dining Room lends a feudal dignity to the warmth of its burnished walnut woodwork and polished marble walls. The floor is inlaid wood, its waxed richness brightly reflecting the 64 concealed light fixtures overhead. Wall tapestries, done in the world's finest needlepoint made in Vienna, tell the deeds of King Arthur.

Dominating the room is the dining table—King Arthur's own renowned Round Table—with each knight's chair in place and with the heraldic shield of the valiant knight who occupies it emblazoned on its back. The dining service is solid gold and each place is set with goblet, plate and wine glasses. A walnut sideboard holds a silver serving tray and Bristol glass decanter and tumblers. Nearby stands a Battersea enamel wine keg. A buffet on the other side displays

Rare woods make up Library floor ⋙→

Castle cookbook—small as a teaspoon

a collection of gold teapots, an ivory chocolate set and a breakfast set of Royal Caldon china, with egg cups the size of the head of a kitchen match.

The doorway on our right leads into the magic kitchen which serves this banquet hall. Mother Goose has claimed this room for her own; and Jack and Jill, Little Jack Horner, Contrary Mary and Little Bo-Peep march around walls painted by Alice O'Neill. On an extraordinary pigmy-sized copper stove hums a tea kettle. This stove, found by the Princess in a Fairyland antique shop, is the one in which the wicked witch locked Hansel and Gretel.

Nearby is a fairy cook book filled with recipes given by some of America's most famous chefs. On a table stands a complete dinner service of Royal Doulton china, each piece bearing the crest of Mary, the late Dowager Queen of England. The dinner plates are as large as a person's thumbnail. And in a cupboard along with the Sevres tea set and the Delft platters are two small amber glasses that were used in every doll house owned by Colleen Moore. One of the prize contents of the kitchen is a set of pewter mugs made for Miss Moore by Thomas F. Owens of the Museum of Science and Industry staff. They are exact copies of Early American pieces, and their handles were carved from wood recovered from the World War II debris of the bombed section of England's Westminster Abbey.

Extra silver as well as bottles filled with fairy wine are stored in a room above the kitchen and reached by a winding stairway in the north wall. In this

Nursery rhymes supply the kitchen's motif ⟫→

room some of the pottery is old, being choice pieces found in Mexico long ago. Some of the glass bottles are from Italy and others from Germany and Mexico.

We must not tarry in this surprising kitchen for we have yet to see the regal bed chambers. They are atop that aerial stairway which beckons us in the great hall. If we can make our feet light enough to surmount this railingless, floating stairway we will find ourselves in the bed chamber of the Fairy Prince. Its deep blue walls and ceiling are relieved with frescoed gold.

THE REGAL CHAMBERS

The theme for the bedroom was set by an old Russian fairy tale wherein a little prince had his arms and legs turned to silver by a wicked witch. If you look closely you will see that the posts at the foot of the bed are figures of the witch, while the headboard is a carved replica of the little boy. Quaint chairs about the room have legs like those of the goat who played an important part in the tale.

A gold mesh screen from China encrusted with jewels masks a balcony that overlooks the hall below. Inside the room are two chests of drawers made in Japan of gold inlaid with iron and silver. They are the products of a family of artisans who have handed down their skills from one generation to another. One chest in the Prince's room is several hundreds of years old while the other was made in Tokyo about 30 years ago, especially for the Fairy Castle. It depicts five famous Japanese fairy tales.

Two small gold cannons stand on one chest, while above on the wall is a collection of swords. Excalibur, the famous sword of King Arthur, is close by. Red seven league boots, just like those they used in Fairyland, stand by an armoire in a corner and near this is the Prince's prie-dieu. It is in front of a painting on copper of the Virgin of Guadalupe, painted by Ramos Martinez, the Mexican artist.

The white bearskin rug that covers the center of the floor posed a problem. Miss Moore took an ermine skin to a taxidermist asking him to fashion the rug like a polar bear with his mouth gleaming with big white teeth, only to hear him say he could make the bear but not with its mouth open. Imagine Miss Moore's surprise when the rug was finished to find the taxidermist had made the bear with its mouth open and filled with white, wicked looking teeth. Asked

Russian fairytale figures adorn bed in Prince's room

where he got the teeth, he told Miss Moore, "I caught a little mouse, took out his teeth and put them in your polar bear."

The adjoining bathroom is done in alabaster. Two reclining mermaids guard the tub while water flows from a sea shell above. The golden lavatory has wee faucets shaped like fish while above hangs a gold mirror set with a sapphire surrounded by diamonds. Once in a ring of her grandmother, it was given to Miss Moore to put in the Fairy Castle.

Also in the bathroom is a gold medicine chest set above another old Japanese chest of drawers, like those in the Prince's bedroom.

Leading from this into a magnificent robing room is a proscenium arch done in plaster decorated with gold.

The bedroom of the Princess, across the entrance hall, has a gossamer air of moonlit fantasy and rose-scented daintiness. The walls are ivory-hued and over a door as we enter we see Peter Pan dancing on a mushroom. The floor is mother-of-pearl with a border of gold. The canopied bed of gold, shaped like a fairy boat and with its golden spider web coverlet, is, of course, the very one where the Sleeping Beauty reposed for 100 years. By its side are seen her golden slippers, as well as her red satin ones, on the tiniest hook rug ever made, and nearby is an ivory spinet, the one on which Rosebud pricked her finger.

On a small ivory dresser is the smallest toilet set in the world. Its brush of gold is only three-quarters of an inch long and is set with diamonds while its bristles are silver fox. There also are a comb, mirror and nail file; and in a gold jewelry box with a crest of diminutive diamonds, lies the Princess' wedding ring. All are the work of Guglielmo Cini, a famous jeweler in Boston.

Two little chandeliers hanging from the ceiling hold six small candles that also are lighted with grain of wheat lights. The pair of diamond and emerald chairs in this room were once dress clips owned by Miss Moore, the outcome of a suggestion by a leading Des Moines jeweler, who told her, "Those clips you are wearing would make beautiful chairs for the Princess."

How expertly he converted them into such priceless showpieces is reflected in the admiration expressed by all who view the Fairy Castle.

The Battersea enamel chairs, footstool and settee were found after years of searching.

←≪ *Golden lions guard the Prince's alabaster bath*

Bed which Sleeping Beauty occupied is found in the Princess' chamber

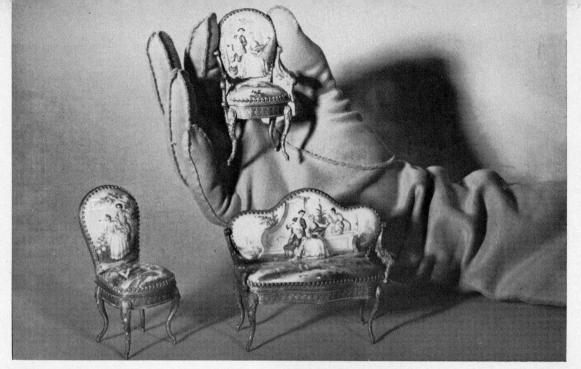

Battersea enamel chairs and settee

Chairs of the Princess were once diamond and emerald dress clips

The world's smallest toilet set

Gold and diamond jewel boxes, smaller than a ring

The Princess' bath is done in crystal and jade and its etched walls tell the story of Undine, the water sprite. Six octagonal pillars of crystal support the ceiling which is glass and etched with butterflies and birds seen flying over the silver fountain-type tub in the center of the floor. The water pouring into the bath comes from the mouths of two silver sea horses which rest on silver sea shells. Perched on the shoulders of the sea horses are two silver cupids. A perfume cabinet of silver adorns the wall above a wash basin made of a silver tulip. The little faucets are also tulip shaped.

A FAIRYLAND CHAPEL

The chapel of this gorgeous Fairyland castle is one of transcendent loveliness. The ceiling is painted from the illuminations in the Book of Kells, that most famous of medieval illuminated manuscripts, now carefully preserved in Dublin, Ireland. The floor, designed by Bayard de Volo, is inlaid with biblical symbols that form a beautiful mosaic.

The stained glass window, a work of Helga Brabon, tells the stories of David and Goliath, Daniel in the Lion's Den, the Finding of Moses, and the Judgment of Solomon. A gold vigil light, with a large diamond scintillating at the top, is set with rubies, sapphires and diamonds which gleam in the light of the six diminutive candles burning at each side. Above it hangs a jeweled icon of the Virgin.

Before the altar are the prie-dieux of the Prince and Princess. On hers rests the smallest Bible in the world and yet containing the entire New Testament. It was printed in 1840. Bound in red leather and gold, it is clasped tight with a gold hinge. On his rests a wee book depicting in woodcuts the lives of the saints. This, too, is an old and rare book. In a glass vial to one side is a carved ivory crucifix, made in Italy over 500 years ago. Though less than a quarter-inch wide, the entire carving is perfect when seen under a magnifying glass.

On a small ivory stand is a bust of Pope Pius IX, one of the most valued items in the castle. Originally, this statuette was the personal seal of Pius IX (the Vatican seal is on the bottom of the bust).

Over the carved altar, guarded by an angel on either side, is "Holy Night," a copy of an oil painting of the Nativity by Correggio; while to the right can be seen the sacristy where a gold baptismal font is placed. Serving as a screen

Water pours constantly into Princess' silver tub

behind this is a fragment of stained glass blown out from Lambeth Palace, residence of the Archbishop of Canterbury, during the blitz of World War II.

The pulpit, with figures of the Apostles, is also to the right of the altar and on its lectern is another Bible decorated with religious scenes of the Old Testament. Off to one side is a gold and ivory organ, carved in Italy with over a hundred keys—each barely a sixteenth of an inch wide. If you are real quiet, you can hear it playing.

THE LIBRARY

Across the garden from the dining room is the library. This is one of the most imaginative and enticing spots in the Castle. Overhead, the copper domed ceiling depicts the constellations. The fireplace is a massive masterpiece in copper and bronze. It is cast as a fish net which, sweeping into the depths of the ocean painted walls, catches in its folds an amused Old Father Neptune and two of his fairest mermaids. A close look at Father Neptune reveals the face of the late, famous motion picture actor Wallace Beery. The andirons are bronze anchors. Ship capstans support the firebox in which magic logs burn merrily. Over the fireplace in full relief and above the fish net is Captain Kidd standing guard over his pirate chests.

Two arched doorways leading into the garden of Aladdin are framed in story book groups. One depicts Gulliver pulling the tiny Lilliputian navy out of the sea, and the other shows Robinson Crusoe on his castaway island with his man, Friday, at his feet. The figures were designed and executed by Harry Jones. At each end of the room tortoise shell steps lead to twin platforms on which rest tiers of books that in themselves are the most fascinating part of this remarkable library.

The bookshelves contain a most unusual library of first editions. To obtain them, Miss Moore had small books made with blank pages. These were given to the authors to write parts of their famous books, making these rare books not merely first editions, but "only" editions. Many of them contain original stories, and each is bound in leather with the author's name embossed in gold.

In the library are personal writings of: A. Conan Doyle, Louis Bromfield, Clare Booth Luce, William Randolph Hearst, Irvin Cobb, Sinclair Lewis, F. Scott Fitzgerald, Booth Tarkington, Lloyd Douglas, Fannie Hurst, Kathleen Norris, John Steinbeck, Carl Van Vechten, James Hilton, Adela Rogers St. Johns,

Edna Ferber, Joseph Hergesheimer, Gene Fowler, Charles Norris, Rupert Hughes, Eleanor Glyn, Robinson Jeffers, Willa Cather, Edgar Rice Burroughs, and Hervey Allen.

Average size of the books is an inch square, although there are several fairy pocket-sized editions, too. A library table holds a postage stamp-sized copy of a magazine and a volume, entitled "The Enchanted Castle," authored by Miss Moore herself.

Among the unusual volumes here is a photographic album of European royalty, and another devoted to famous movie stars.

Also in this fairy library are small antique books, printed from type in the years 1820 to 1900, and there is an unusual album which could well be called an autographic history of our times. Its pages show signatures of such famous people as Franklin D. Roosevelt, Nehru, Churchill, de Gaulle, Toscanini, and Henry Ford. Each signature represents a person who has contributed to Twentieth Century progress. Others whose signatures appear are: General Eisenhower, General Pershing, Admiral Byrd of South Pole fame, the Duke and Duchess of Windsor, Queen Elizabeth II, the Crown Prince of Japan, and Paderewski, first Premier of Poland.

The furniture of this extraordinary room was designed for equally extraordinary readers. Fairy folk seem to assume the most peculiar positions when they read.

Here, for example, is a curiously shaped settee, made of a greenish copper shell resting on sea horses. It is an ideal "tummy-reading chair" for little leprechauns who prefer to read lying on their convex stomachs. There is another sofa for a Prince who likes to peruse his books while leaning on his left elbow, a matching sofa for one who likes to rest on his right elbow, and still another for Fairyland readers who like to lie on their backs with their feet in the air for getting the fullest enjoyment out of their reading. Fairies are acrobatic folk, so the designer of these peculiar lounges prepared for even the most eccentric.

Between the library and the chapel is a small passageway whose only decoration is a whimsical mural done by Alice O'Neill, entitled "Love in Bloom." It depicts the adventures of a few of the passengers of Noah's Ark, who are seen debarking in a long line of amorous couplets. There are a pair of affectionate giraffes, one of which has the languorous eyelashes of a Mata Hari, a pair of crocodiles romantically snapping at each other, and two formal penguins who are strolling off demurely along with all the other animal passengers of that famous watery voyage.

TREASURE—JEWELS—FAIRY KNICKKNACKS

Above the passageway, on the next floor and reached only by an iron bound trap door, is the treasure room. With barred windows, and guarded by Ali Baba who mastered the Forty Thieves, the treasure room holds vast quantities of fairy loot, such as souvenirs of famous Fairyland parties, antique charms, love potions in jeweled decanters, rings of enchantment and the abracadabra of sorcery.

It is impossible to begin to describe the hundreds of other beautiful creations so many craftsmen have contributed to make the interior of the Fairy Castle a wonderland in every detail; but, before we leave and resume our normal size, let us walk for a moment along the paths of the enchanted garden lying beneath its inner battlements. Here we see fountains shooting constant streams of silvery water upward toward the branches of fairy trees; here we hear the golden melodies of the feathered nightingale; here will be found Cinderella's silver coach drawn by four silver horses which have halted for a minute to drink from a coppery fountain; and here stand the weeping willow tree that really weeps and another tree in which "rock-a-bye baby" is seen actually being rocked. The weeping tree's branches are piped for water and it cries all day.

Looking up toward the castle's turrets, we can discern the figures from the Wizard of Oz that adorn the walls and, high above, Santa Claus and his sled drawn by his faithful reindeer and sweeping over the steeples of this idyllic domain.

Yet, with all of its rare treasures, this fabulous and colorful Fairy Castle seems to lack one thing. Hundreds of otherwise awe-struck visitors voice the frequently asked question: "Where are the fairies; where are the Prince and Princess who live here?"

Those who are lucky have seen them. Perhaps this is only an illusion, but those who have seen them will tell you exactly what they look like; how they are dressed; and, because enchantment plays such a part, it is not strange that each story is different. After all, this Fairy Castle and all fairy castles are peopled with the fairies of your childhood dreams.

Such is the magic of Fairyland.